PRAISE FOR AFTERGLOW

Afterglow is a poetic eruption of cosmic salvation. Each poem is a sacred coordinate along a stardust pathway toward heroic healing. Wynter's poetry propels us along the revolutionary voyage of reclaiming the self no matter the scars that have shaped us. *Afterglow* is a poetry collection that does not hold back. Instead, Wynter rallies us to rise up and stand firm in our divine magic, where our courageous faith in self radiates the most beautiful essence of who we were meant to be.

— *Alex Petunia, author of* Tending My Wild

•

Wynter Eddins speaks the truth. She takes the reader into a journey of pain and dysfunction. She paints the picture of children holding onto secrets as adults continue to lie and betray their innocence. The beauty of Wynter's work is she does not leave the reader in the pain, she gives this little girl a voice, and one day she gains the strength to stand tall and speak. She then advocates for others and no longer stays quiet. In this work, Wynter gives voice to those who are too afraid to speak. This book is for every woman, every man, and every child who was robbed of their childhood through family trauma. She gives hope that the hurt can no longer define us, and with healing we can rise and give the gift of empowerment to others through our example.

— *Erica Castro, author, speaker, life coach, educator*

•

Afterglow is a transformative voyage of the heart set against an expansive galactic backdrop. Wynter's words beautifully navigate the journey of a heart that bleeds, scars, and finally emerges, mended and open to "wishes" once more. This work gives a voice to the silent stories of Black women who have endured the harrowing experiences of sexual trauma and domestic violence. As I embarked on Wynter's journey, I felt seen, heard, ready to face my trauma, and take on the stars.

— *Tyler Lenn Bradley, motivational poet*

AFTERGLOW

~~after~~
GLOW

One Star's Ending Is a Black Woman's Beginning

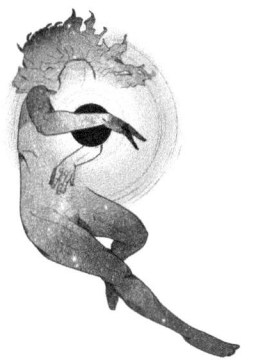

WYNTER L. EDDINS

World Stage Press
Verse from the Village

World Stage Press
Verse from the Village

Afterglow
©2023 Wynter L. Eddins
ISBN: 978-1-952952-54-8

First Edition, 2023

All rights reserved. No part of this publication may be reproduced, distributed, or transmitted in any form or by any means, including photocopying, recording, or other electronic or mechanical methods, without the prior written permission of the publisher, except in the case of brief quotations embodied in critical reviews and certain other noncommercial uses permitted by copyright law.

Printed in the United States of America

Cover Design by Adam Martinez & Emily Anne Evans
Layout Design by Eswari Kamireddy & Emily Anne Evans

For every explorer who looks to the stars and sees infinite possibilities.
For every survivor who ever once questioned their worth.
You are needed.

And for all those beautiful souls whose spirits call out for justice, you will always be remembered — your stories will forever be honored:

- ★ Breonna Taylor, 26
- ★ Yong Ae Yue, 63
- ★ Sandra Bland, 28
- ★ Vanessa Guillén, 20
- ★ Breasia Terrell, 10
- ★ Xiaojie Tan, 49
- ★ Tioni Theus, 16
- ★ Sarayah Jade Redmond, 19
- ★ Delaina Ashley Yaun, 33
- ★ For all women and children who have suffered at the hands of violence
- ★ For all Missing and Murdered Indigenous Women (MMIW)
- ★ For all women and children who have lost their lives at the hands of violence
- ★ For all those who suffered from mental illness and lost their lives
- ★ For all people who endured or suffered any loss from violence in their community

CONTENTS

Acknowledgments	xii
Preface	xv

OUTER EVENT HORIZON

Stay*	7
Shush!*	9
Private Sector*	11
A Nebulous Vacuum	13
Atypical Invasion	16
Heart Lesson	17
Cowardly Tale*	18
Soul Scale	19
Unturned Bones*	21
Gallery of Lies	24
Excavation	26
Distance*	28
Resist	30
Distant Learning	31
Habitat Untamed	32
A Letter to the Broken Parts	33
Darkmatter*	34
Case Cold Memories*	36

* Content Warning: These poems reference sexual assault and domestic violence.

INNER EVENT HORIZON

Cosmic Comfort	41
Blast Off	42
Rare Discovery	43

Dead Zone	45
Grandfather	46
Dirtsider	48
Theme Song	50
Energy	52
Student Equation	54
Signal Truth	56
First	58
Solar Send	59
Dewless Days	61
Crawl Space	64

SINGULARITY

Acts of Gratitude	71
Infinite Love	72
Illuminate	74
Warmest Star	75
Morning Wealth	76
Peace to Will	78
Barrier Matter	80
Infinite Connection	82
Steer North	83
Galactic Moves	84
Wild. Honey. Nectar.	85
Cosmic Forces	86
Start Energy	88
Spacelift	91
Universal Blessings	93
Macrocosmic Might	94
Celestial Rebirth	97
Earth Bounty	98
Land Sleep	100

First Steps	101
Rocketry	103
Light Protector	104
Shooting Star	107
Sword Fight	108
Inner Compass	110
Screen Glory	111
Super Martians	113
Seismic Shift	114
Starburst	116
Intergalactic Community	117
Radiated Pressure	119
Lethargy	121
Roomy	123
Believe	125
Cosmic Resistance	127
North Star	128

ACKNOWLEDGMENTS

I am thankful to be surrounded by an amazing support group. Thank you, Jesus, for being my Guide, the Redeemer. I am forever humbled by Your Grace. Thank you to the CLI community, World Stage Press, Hiram Sims, and the Infinite Poets, who are my family and who helped to create masterpieces together. My partner in the poetry community, Tyler Bradley, and teacher, Alex Petunia, whose dedication to support others in poetry is unmatched.

A huge thank you to my beautiful mother, who shows up for every one of my adventures — your unwavering love for your children does not go unnoticed. My father, for always finding a way to make it to all of my spoken word performances, cheering me on ever since I got into the art. To my brothers, Justyn, LB, Malachi, Elijah, thank you for always having my back. Thank you to my beautiful sister, Aysia Turner, the way you live your life in truth is something that truly inspires me. To my cousin Delia and my best friend Fan Jie for always reminding me of my worth by being so genuine, I could not have gotten here without you all.

My heart is immensely grateful to my nonprofit team at Simply Youth Institute (SYI), who have always worked humbly to create safe spaces, and educate young women in our Los Angeles community about financial responsibility, career exploration, and confidence. Many pieces of this collection stem from the work we do with SYI. To all the amazing educators, I love you, and you are superheroes in the community.

Thank you to Sojourner Truth, an American abolitionist, whose story of resilience and unshakable faith inspired two pieces in this collection titled "Steer North" and "Inner Compass." I want to thank my church community, Grace United Methodist Church, Los Angeles, and the pastors and members who I have known throughout the years and who have become more like family. We are more than conquerors and expect great things through Jesus Christ our Lord.

I am grateful for all of the students I had the honor to work with and who saw the best in me and believed in my passion for the arts as much as I believed in their dreams. I pray they become the leaders and changemakers I know they can be for their community.

Finally, I am thankful to you, for choosing to read the *Afterglow* limited collection.

PREFACE

Dear Space Traveler,

Imagine every moment, all celebrations, love, loss, pain, and hurt, collapsed into itself — that is how this collection was born.

Afterglow represents an inner and outer survival journey, layered with all its complexities and simplicities. Each of our life experiences brought us to where we are today. We weathered through storms — domestic violence, child sexual trauma — that were out of this world, unspeakable, and unbelievable life events. *Afterglow* is an examination of existence as a supernova black hole where gravity is so strong that nothing — not even pain and hurt — can escape it. This collection shines light on violence against women. I cannot forget the horrific stories of violence that robbed innocent women of color from living out their full and healthy lives.

Personal experiences create an inevitable reality. However, life presents infinite possibilities when we embrace all of ourselves. In the past, I refused to face my trauma, weighed down by shame and feelings of unworthiness.

After I accepted the love of Jesus Christ into my heart, I discovered the roots of grace grow infinitely, and the gravity of light is inescapable. **We must own who we are** and be proud of our innermost scars, no matter how deeply they run. Doing so opens a path toward healing, a path filled with mysteries and faith untold.

There is so much mystery inside a black hole that no one truly knows about all the phenomena that occurs within. It is the same with faith, stuck in the duality between feeling uncomfortable and comfortable. Understanding that all answers aren't apparent but trusting faith, which can feel massive, overwhelming at times, will always lead to renewal and restoration. Trust requires so much selfless love that it evolves into a beautiful mass which defies time and space.

Afterglow is a safe and infinite place to be oneself, **never letting the light of God's love escape** — this is where we all must live. This is where we all must give and receive, a place that is deeply filled with a pull for community like no other.

Let's embark together,
Wynter L. Eddins

~~after~~ GLOW

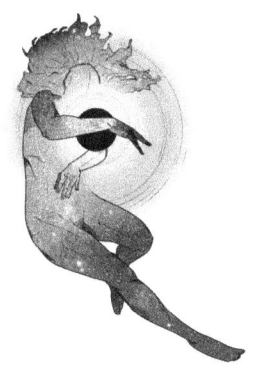

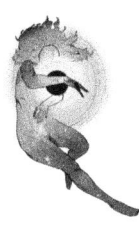

WELCOME, SPACE TRAVELER.

I am nervous to reveal the distant parts of me, which are still that — a part of me. It's interesting how childhood sexual trauma can have lasting effects. After I was sexually assaulted at eight years old, I experienced a disconnection that left permanence on my body and my soul. Interlaced in my galaxy of womanhood, I felt I was at a point of no return — that I could never erase the gut-wrenching pain.

I was wrong.

Afterglow begins with **the point of no return** — the darkness that can seem like it will never disappear, a swallow into a hole that feels impossible to escape. I say often that **poetry saved my life** — it urged me to acknowledge the pain. When traumatic events occur, oftentimes there are no words to describe the amount of hurt that persists. Growing up in a Black American family, those uncomfortable conversations about sexual assault were unwelcomed. I felt "dirty," and I was ashamed to address such topics. The harmful idea that protecting the abuser somehow protects the family is outdated and broken, and it seeks to perpetuate the harm while the offender does not have an opportunity to take accountability and seek redemption — thus resulting in a fragmented family unit.

These toxic and rejectable notions were brought to the **outer horizon**.

You are entering the point of no return — no matter how painful it is to read about.

A gentle reminder to **put your needs first**. Prioritize your health and feel empowered to skip anything that could be a negative trigger. At the point of no return, you are able to bend time and space as you see fit. You are in control here, and it is you who will decide how thorough to explore this part of my collapsed star.

We are arriving in 3...2...1

Tread carefully,
Wynter L. Eddins

Part 1:
OUTER EVENT HORIZON

Stay

There is
no moving on.
Only moving past.
The past holds on.
The pain still lasts.

There is
no moving on from
what happened that night.
Pieces of her still scattered.
Closed lips sealed tight.

There is
no moving on from
one's broken trust.
Boundaries evaded. To
act on one's own lust.

There is
no moving on.
Trauma's lullaby.

Singing hurtful melodies as
time flies by.

Body grows.
Heart tries to recover. But
her mind still knows. Her
soul a cautious lover.

What
happened a long time ago
feels like yesterday's news.
Fresh off the presses. Ink turns
blue.

There is
no moving on.
No such thing as being strong.
Dealing with the day-to-day.
And just getting along.

There is
no moving on.

Shush!

My deepest, darkest secret was plunged
into the depths of family business.

Shoved into the pockets of
"Can you keep a secret?"
Swept into the corners of
"You better not tell"
and wrapped up tightly in an airtight
container labeled:

Black families don't share family business.

My mouth sealed shut, closed to the truth. He
still wants to play hide-and-seek. I hide, hoping
one day he won't find me. Cornered
in my home, he always finds me alone.
White shirt starched, drenched in sweat.

Mama asks, "Where's your pants, girl?"
I want to tell Mama my deepest, darkest secret.
But it is buried
in the mud of "Shush! That was a long time ago,"
so I keep on. One day,
I will tell dad; he will crumble. But
for now, I show up at school confused as hell, too.
Who can I tell?

No one.

No one can know how my soul left
me that night, a balled up piece of paper,
call it what you like. I rock back
every night, hoping they do not invite him
again. But the doorbell rings
and I hear him walk in.

Hide-and-seek, he always finds me
alone in my home.

My deepest, darkest secret
was melted down into
 "It's no big deal. This happens all the time. You will heal."

So I push on.
I'm in high school now, confused as hell.
Let them all have me,
worthless pieces of my body.
Let them all have me.
For who I am is not who I wish to be.

I wish to tell my deepest, darkest secret to my family.
Stretched and worn out,
erosion is beginning to show
on my day-to-day whereabouts.

Who can I tell my deepest, darkest secret to?

It's beginning to feel like hands raised all day,
waving in the air.
Can anyone see me?
I look around and everyone's there.
Mama and Pops, brothers, too.
I tell them my deepest, darkest secret

and now they know my truth.

Private Sector

Family matters.
Private business.
Cannot share it.
Mind your business.

Don't tell nobody.

Family matters.
On the stage.
Behind scenes
An open cage.

I was a nasty little boy.

Family matters.
Secrets too,
Bury them deep.
Erase the rule.

I am different now.

Family matters.
Wasted shame.
Silence creeps.
Point the blame.

Why are you bringing this up?

Family matters.
Pull the blinds.
Close the door.
Enjoy your time.

I thought you liked it.

Family matters.
Keep it close.
If hurt is love,
Then you're loved the most.

We used to be close.

Family matters.
Spend the night.
If he comes.
Well that's a fright.

I don't understand why you told on me.

Family matters.
To Little ones
Robbed of innocence.
Told to shush.

Family shatters.

I climbed in just that once.

Nebulous Vacuum

Fill her up
and solve her
mystery.
Don't let her
feel pity. Pits
of grief are to be
filled.

Good deeds.
Money.
Scholarships.
Diversity.
Inclusion.

She
cries for these things. Then
lies about their success. There
are no answers to her test.
She is
empty.

A barrel filled
with good intentions.
Harvested carefully
with good mentions.
To challenge her
is to doubt her
good sense.

She
believes she knows better.
Better than those
she wants to help. So
she speaks for them, says

they can't
speak for themselves.
Save them.
She promises.

Don't name them.

They're all the same.
Their experiences are
identical twins.
Their hopes and dreams are
mirrors of reflection.
She promises
ultimate protection.

Trust her good nature.
Her policies are
interventional saviors.
She shines
the light to follow.
Those who turn from it have
trouble tomorrow.

Better yet —
she is the only way.

Her truth
turns gray.
Her truth
turns white.
Her truth turns
into nothingness.

Flight.

Agency is the
only truth to seek.
Ownership is the
only way to be.
Freedom comes from
one place:

The battle for **REAL** democracy.

Atypical Invasion

Wash over me
like a cold ocean wave.

Negative thoughts
pierce me,
invade and conquer.

Set up ship and
raise their alien flag.

I surrender.

Hands behind
bowed head.

Have mercy.

Stabbed in the heart.
Eyes flush white.

Body jerks.

Fear
won the fight.

Heart Lesson

Wanted to go through and get some,
now feeling slighted.
Like a different ending was to come.

Eyes were softer,
lips, too.
Maybe this time
he'd be into you.

He'd look right through,
even try to
see something more.

He might even restore.
Reset.

Thought this was it.
That's why the hips let him in.
They told him to begin,
hard always inside.

He lost his mind —
mine, too.

Now I can't see you.
You can't see me.

I brought you to God.
His silence was an answer
I refused to let be.

Now I am standing alone
because I refused to see.
I refused to listen.

Hard lessons
are the ones you give in.

Cowardly Tale

Too bad you ran away that day.
Too bad you cowered away.
Too bad for you, lucky for me.

Devil tried to make a family.

Truth revealed you had no soul.
Tried to take another's, though.
Given that your hands were tight.
Choked a neck then slept alright.

Too bad you ran away that day.
Too bad you even looked my way.
Too bad they caught you, lucky for me.

The thought of you captured my heart, you see.
Evil tried to chase me down.

Reported him, he ran out of town.
Must hide and lurk in the shadows
each day.
Like devils do, his back never turned away.

Too bad you ran away that day.
Too bad you are still free to stay.
Too bad for you, lucky for me.

I changed my path.

My destiny.

Soul Scale

What is a life worth?

Measured in
papers, signed on
dotted lines.
No assurance for the
insurance policy.
Canceled
moments before.

What is a life worth?

If healthcare bills compromise
most of our debt?
And the sick are suffering from
flat-out neglect.

Collectors still collecting.
Taxes being raised. But
if the youth cannot read,
systems do not change.

What is a life worth?

Funding for schools. Families
starving next door. But
these are the rules.

Written in blood,
let them thirst.

Prices will rise again.
Rich will grow richer.
Who will win? Who will win?

What is a life worth?

When sexual violence is
silenced.
Transgressions are
swept away.

Survivors left to weep.
Abusers set free.
Part of her still broken.

No need for sympathy.

What is a life worth?

I will tell you now.
Life is priceless.
Immeasurable.

Worthy of praise.
Worthy of happiness.
Worthy of better days.

Unturned Bones

Stood in front of a
dark, open mouth, waiting
to swallow me whole — or else.

I cannot step

into this unbeknownst hell.
One more step, I will shatter.
Shame adorns my head.

I wear it.

Lord, who gives names
to the dead?

I do.

I cannot forget
the stones unturned.
Buried, I yearn for answers

in the night
when I dream of her.
The pain she felt

is mine.

Now I stand,
ready to enter.
Almost.

If I go in,
I do not know what
I will find.

Her bones, they are mine.

Stretched out and
spread in unfound spaces.
This can't be the place

I was born into.

Someone
tell me to wake
from the truth.

Ruthlessness.

I cannot accept the
cruelty inside.
How hearts despise lives.

I cannot comprehend evil.
Hate. Numbness.
Unsolved mysteries.

I must first reject my own.

I know much more than I want to.
Darkness lives around every bone.
Marrow can be eaten.
People kill without reason.

This is the world we live in.

Her nakedness bears my soul.
Hard to accept such ugliness.
Spewed out all over,

blood is spilling.

I hear her screams at night.
Even when I am kneeling,
praying to the One

who may shed light.

Why did this happen?
Words cannot respond.
I am sickened to see.

Now I stand at the mouth, ready
to jump straight into
the monster's heart.

I know I will find answers.

There, I will start.

Gallery of Lies

I have stepped in dark places
and traced it back to this moment.

Looking at the path
awakened my spirit to calm down,
and recognize
the lies society wrapped in golden cloaks,
and feel-good strokes
with sparkling diamonds.

A lie I am lying in.

With others, I followed along to fit in and belong.
I tried so hard to fall without scraped knees, blackened eyes.
That was me back then, in dark places.
I traced them to this moment.

How am I standing tall
when I could so easily fall back down?

Back to shaving inches off my life,
each shot, each time I lied to protect those
who could not care less if I survived.
Back to his hand and following all his demands.

Back to pity and wallowing in self-shame.

I could fall back to those times
when I could not see between blurred lines,
but how could I?

The cycle of control is relentless,
it results in bloody stitches
and lives lost.
The cost is unlimited, with no take-backs.
No let's retrack.
I must pay with my life.

The power is the lock
and the key is the control.

This, I know.

Excavation

Her voice is buried deep
under the ocean's crest. Sank
there that day as
she lay on her breast.
Her heart and rib cage
pressed against the ground.
Her voice drowned.

She found herself stressed.
Her heart
and soul pressed.
No sound came.

She remembers
her mind running,
her body pinned down.
No one is coming for her
this time around.

This is the night.

Her eyes were flashing,
signs of terrible fright.
She could not flee,
she could not
save her voice.
The one who saved me.

She let it go, she
watched it sink all the way down.
How far her voice drowned,
a million depths into the sea.

That day,
she lost her integrity.
That day,
she lost her agency.

Her voice buried among
watery treasuries,
never to be found.
Chained away,
stuck and anchored
to the ocean ground.

In time,
she would again discover it.
One day, she would recover it.
She would dig it up.

Refill her soul cup.

Distance

Tickles up my spine.
I am naked this time.
Crawling skin.

I can't fake it.
My toes are tight.
Twisted.
My soul feels like
it will shatter again.

Feels like
my skin will crawl into itself.
Explode,
when I feel the tickling tail
of soft touch.

Fingers prodding
in uninvited spaces.
Destroying, penetrating,
so deep.

I see RED.
I see BLACK.
I DON'T SEE

ANYTHING.

I like it like that.

I remember my face at that moment.
How I knew it wasn't right.
His lustful games took away my rite.

Never knew
a path to womanhood
could feel so blight, so contrite.

Robbed, an unsolved heist.
Broke into my temple,
disappeared into the night.

Resist

Are you tired of the siege upon your soul?
How far more to go?
The road is rough.
Your feet are tough and bruised.
You can no longer choose the direction.
Instead, you stand at the intersection.

Ever felt like giving in?
Like the weight of the world is dented in,
and you are stuck holding both ends,
waiting for the planet to crash and spin.
Ever felt like disappearing?
Melting into the walls and staring
blankly, from a distance.
The horizon is distant.

Too far to reach.

Ever felt like letting go?
Throwing it all in the fire, then the snow.
Freezing it, till you've burned your heart.
Ever felt like falling apart?
Forgetting the pieces,
letting them scatter.
Diseases without cures,
only if there were fewer.

Ever felt like standing tall?
Like giving it your all?
Like leaving it on the table.
Being able to partake in
a handshake, a hug.
Giving all the love,
not expecting any in return.

Selfless heart, this we yearn.

Distant Learning

Home alone. Again.
Time to log in.
Computer won't charge.
My heart is enlarged.

I feel anxious.

Teachers demand I am on time.
Online. I hate it.
I feel I can't escape it.
Barely awake.
They ask me to partake
in discussion.

They can't see me.
If I turn off my camera, see.
Where are you?
Teacher calls out my name.
Says if I don't answer,
then it's me to blame.

Alone in my home. Again.
No more school.
It seems just a dream.
Pressing keys and doing things.
What have I learned this year?
I couldn't tell you.

I'm stuck in fear.

Anxious about whether or not
I will get to enter the lot.

See my teachers. See my friends.
Maybe never. Never again.

#pandemiclife

Habitat Untamed

A habitat not built for a slithering tail.
Curiosity chased away by the veil.
Covered ceilings kept out the light.
A habitat not built for the scurries,
not built for a demeanor hurried.
The investigator,
the cocked head.

It is dark in this place, the dread.
The willingness to stay with no chase.
Habitat did not fit the one
with two eyes on the face.
A belly
filled with captured regrets.
Never empty, never full.
Forced to live in a place with no hue.

Glass breaks.

So many tails are
leaving the confined space
to their natural habitat
filled with green serene
flies to fill the belly's dream
with freedom on the horizon.
A chance to enliven.

Leaving behind
the cage.
Leaving behind
the rage.

A habitat untamed
is the lizard's name.

A Letter to the Broken Parts

Dear Heart,

You are bleeding again. Blood is spilling to no end and this time I won't be able to stop it. Remember when I patched you up? I stayed up all night to make sure you had the love, the protection, the aide. I put the bandage on you and kissed you goodnight. I hope you remember that sight. I said to be careful next time around.

Don't let them smash you on the ground. Don't let them toss you aside, and dismiss you. Don't you dare hide. But don't be so brave. Maybe I confused you… Is that why you stayed in the same places that caused you such pain? I never intended for you to be so damaged. Now you are bleeding again, and this time I don't have the tools to heal and mend.

You are asking me to do things that are out of my hands. You beat yourself down and you expect me to begin again, to forget that I wiped your tears. I spent all of my time, sewing pieces of you back together. I labeled them "fragile-like," wrapped in bubble paper and once again said goodnight. You promised me you would tread carefully. Not give yourself to the first one you see, not let them take from you like they tried to take from me. I am guarded. Why are you so free? I am at a loss — your pain, your suffering, too much it cost. I can no longer pretend.

I am sorry to say but, my precious heart, this is the end. Bleed out.

Regretfully,
Your Body

Darkmatter

Erase these gray lines.

Too many times the line was crossed.
Passed off as slightly okay.
She should have pushed him away.
Why didn't she say it till today?

That's a gray area, they say.

He was in the right, too. She knew
what he wanted to do.
So why did she play along?
Why did she scream
inside and not out?
Isn't she strong?

That's a gray area, they say.

But gray lines
do not exist here.
Hear her screams.
She told everything
without saying a word.
But since she was not
singing like a bird.

That's a gray area, they say.

Let her die there. Let her
lose her mind there.
Bury her
in that gray space.
She has no face,
just another number
who did not say NO out loud.

That's a gray area, they say.

Those gray areas
are justified lies.
Her experiences
are real.
Colored in lines.

She deserves
to heal. To live in full color,
not a gray scale.

She will not be erased.

Case Cold Memories

Eventually,
we will all return to dust.

Let it settle
into
silence.
Silos.
The coldness
of you beneath me.

Frozen pieces
still stuck in time.
Innocence
trapped forever.
Fairy tales
turned to Neverlands.

New blooms
picked prematurely.
Petals
barely sticking out.
Squeezed
out by withering weeds.
Greedy
in their pursuit to
devour.

Eventually,
we will all return to dust.

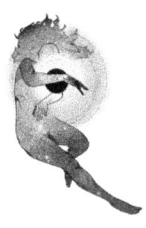

DEAR SPACE TRAVELER,

Congratulations! We are now leaving the past in the past, and will not allow space for the past to dictate our actions and thoughts in the now as we venture toward acceptance.

I have grown into **empowered acceptance**. Empowered acceptance means bringing complete awareness to and shedding light on all the past hurt. By doing so, full awareness sets a reminder that these experiences do not and will not hold any power, and the power these traumatic experiences once held has melted away by acknowledging they happened and are no longer happening now. With that, acceptance opens up a safe space for true spiritual growth. I found reassurance in my faith, letting God's light fill my spirit and empower me to move with a calmness and serenity unlike any feeling I ever experienced. **This is the true gift of grace, an invaluable and immeasurable gift.**

As you explore, I hope you no longer let the past dictate your actions and decisions. Instead, I hope you can accept the past and replace all things considered failure with growth and development.

Empowered acceptance,
Wynter L. Eddins

Part 2:
INNER EVENT HORIZON

Cosmic Comfort

It is a release
to say goodbye
to the pain, to the lies.
It is a release
to say goodbye
to the issues, to the cries.
It is a release
to say goodbye.

To the fakeness, to the strife.
To keep face
when you want to cry.
It is a release
to say goodbye.

To toxicity
in the family.
To unhealthy
relationships.
To the gravity
that held you down.

In all of the spaces.
It is a release
to say goodbye.
To the attitude of
negativity.
To too much
positivity.
To the comfort in
pain.
It is a release
to say goodbye.

Wave. Wave.

Goodbye.

Blast Off

The deeper we go,
the better. Your eyes
are searching inside. My mind
feels like staying alive
in this cold,
harsh world that spins.
Even when
we feel like giving in.
Even when
we feel like stopping short.
There is no pause
button of sorts. We must

continue on.

It feels better
when I belong to you.
I know you cannot
claim me forever,
but just to know
we are together
I am reassured. I have
found love. I could last
on this feeling from above. Like a
precious, rare stone, I will

hold on.

Rare Discovery

Who is she
if she cannot see her reflection?
Shadows hide from
the power she contains.

The wholeness
that is within her
has shattered. She still holds
all the pieces.

They lie
in dark places
she has yet to visit for some time.
Thinking of the distance traveled
is not worth her mind. To take
the pieces back and
sew herself together.

It is a daunting task

She does not wish
to embark on anytime soon,
so she stays in the shadows.
She remembers those places
she could visit with
fearlessness. Now seems
like a distant memory.
Her power
is trapped in a frame.

How can she
turn back the clocks? Back then,
she could unlock any door
and step right through it. Now
her feet are sinking deep.
She can't get through it.

She is stuck.

She did not need anyone
to measure her worth.
She knew.
She used to know.
She remembers now.
A far-off idea of who she was.

A legend
she read about
in the chapter books of her mind.

She gets lost there.

Pages have been torn out,
tethered, edges are half-burned.
She finds comfort in painful memories.
The pleasure of her own sound mind
sounds insane.

She rejects it.

She will find the courage
to look down that familiar road,
to reclaim her own.

One day.
One day.

She will know.

Dead Zone

Wash away
what is left inside.
Enveloping swell
is an ocean tide.

Wash away
what remains of me.
Fill me up with
something new.
Keep me there,
I feel renewed.

Blessings
come from delaying.
Hold still,
avoid staying in pits
that keep the dead alive.

I am walking
into the light.
I see things
so newly bright.
Meet me there,
this time it's right.

Grandfather

I wish I met you.

Grief is so strange.
How can I claim
I knew you?
Life brings pain.
Squeezed out
lemon juice on open cuts.
This is the truth of our existence.
Did I mention?

I wish I met you.

Entrepreneurial mindset,
you did not neglect
your family's needs.
Good deeds,
delivered
with the intention,
to give more.
Did I mention?

I wish I met you.

Cool stride.
Forgiving soul.
The one who had great times.
You never let go. The
deliverance. Your existence.
A treasure chest. Buried
deep in the oceans crest.
I found you there.

I wish I met you.

I'd have called you
Grandpa.
I'd have called you
Pops.
Papa JB, I wish I got to
meet you.

But since I cannot, I will
cherish your memories. Hold
tight to your stories,
told and retold. I will
reclaim them as mine.

For you were someone
I wish I knew
in my lifetime.

Dirtsider

The distance between us
cannot last.
When I travel to your galaxy,
I forget the past.

Transgressions are
transformed into lessons.
Grudges
melted down into tiny pieces.
Crushed
under your solar wind.
Gravity
no longer exists
and I can no longer pretend.

You were always the one.

But I explored planets
until there were none left to see.
I climbed
up every mountain
shook down every tree.

To escape you.

The death of your star took me under,
sucked me in too far.
Black hole.
Quasar.
Lost me. As I

lost you, too.
I searched for you.
I can no longer do
without your shine.
Be mine.
Be mine.
Be mine.

Lost in your space.

For infinite time.

Theme Song

her songs are
blackened keys, pressed
melodies, tuning, playing,
strumming her heart
for better days,
better ways
to keep moving

she is slowly losing,
shedding exterior,

inferiority to majority,
dissipated,
she longs to feel
elevated,
dedication to music
is all she knows, she continues
to practice, stronger
she grows

like a structure untouched,
rising above
glass windows, reinforced
hard metals,
barriers of love
guarded for protection
of her inner dreams,
she longs for all to see

those who discourage
the mission she began,
she resisted
with raised fist that stands
still in the air and sun,
mirrors drawing her near
holding her own gaze
as she tilts her head to the side, barely
recognizing her beautiful stride.

pushing through pages,
standing on stages
she has found her own voice,
a harmonious reflection
of her own inner choice.

Energy

Our heart sings
when it is moving. When we are
grooving through and out.
Our heart dances
and we shout. When we have
a spark inside,
ready to ignite.

Give yourself
all that you have.
Demand
nothing less.
Life is but a test
to measure your abilities. Believe
inside you are still alive.

Find the nerve. Use
all your talents to serve.
Don't try to hide it. Everyone
is waiting to see. But
not everyone has dignity.

Keep it, your integrity.
Hold tight, for it's hard to be.
When you are alone,
do the doubts creep in?
Do they moan and groan?
Telling you to give in?

A lie, press on and try.
Just make it through.
Believe you are right. You
have the right to move on.

To protect
your heart and soul song.
Sing it,
let it fill the room. Let them
dance to your beat. Or
leave the Zoom.

You will find light. When you
sit still inside and listen. The
difficult part is attention. And
being able to dedicate it all.

Are you willing to
sacrifice and fall?
Are you willing to
get back up and call
out to the mountain tops?
Let them ring. Hear
your heart sing.

It calls for
unity and pride.
It calls for
a community alive.
It calls for
service and love.

When the heart sings,
it's a call from
above.

Student Equation

Maybe we lead them
to the well of good decisions.
The more pressure we put on them,
the more incisions. More
reasons to reject the voice of "treason."

Maybe we embrace them
with tougher love.
Give them hard work,
never enough.
Sense of priority
in the community.

Maybe we speak to them
directly. With empathy,
with a call to action.
Maybe we stop relaxin'
on "they're just kids."

No.

They play a role
in all the scenes.
Stop believing in the idea of
"one day they'll grow up."
Make space for them
to show up.

Now.

Include their voices,
reflect on their choices.
Have real consequences.
Community service
needs them all.
Don't let them
fall to the wayside.

Instead —
let them pick up the streets.
See homelessness.
Find their own way to be.
Stop pushing them
down a traditional path.

Let them find solutions,
solve life's graph.

Signal Truth

Sirens are
roaring again.
Calls of urgency are
pressing in.
Hearts are stirring,
awakening inside.

        Eyes are opening,
        brains filling wide.
        Voids of helplessness
        replaced with eagerness
        to show pride.

                To lift each other,
                take one another's full side. No
                dependence is independence.
                Shame is ridden when the
                game is ended.
                To redeem the lost cause.
                The ball is out of bounds.
                No more fouls.
                Shots are taken by
                the team from out of town.
                No longer.

Sirens are
roaring again.
Blaring with drums that call for
readiness and self-development.
The key to the
element is togetherness.
The key is the
rejection of otherness.

        The key is to
        turn it backward and
        break the locks.
        The chains are
        still on and caught in an interweb, stuck.
        Inertia caused the sirens to go off.

                Sirens are
                roaring again.
                Will we move from
                victimization?
                Or let otherness
                be a vein of this nation?

First

If life comes
too fast, slow down
quickly. Press
the brake. Stop the
timer. Don't be too late.
Don't show up early.
Be right on time.

If life comes
too fast, spend
the dime. Hope it lands
face up. Don't make
bets. You can't pay up.
Don't go into
debt. Try to keep up.

If life comes
too fast,
keep dreaming.
Keep believing
you can. No more hard
demands. Protect
your soul. Get the best
deal. Quench your thirst.

If life comes
too fast,
at least
you'll be
first.

Solar Send

Deliver me,
I used to say. There
is no way
but out.
Disappear.
Be invisible.
Live in fear.

Deliver me
from myself,
my wicked ways,
I used to say.
Shame was my guide.
My cane
to lean on.
My only rite.

Deliver me.
Guide me through.
Justify the wrong, so I
can see my truth.
I used to
keep secrets.
Dark ones, too.

Deliver me
like a package left
on doorsteps. To
be opened and
discarded.
Let them have
my heart
and eat it, too. That's
all I knew.

Deliver me. Keep
me in place. Don't
let me wander.
I want to stay
in warm places
where comfort lives.

This time,
I will give
to myself
what I robbed
from myself.
I will return.

Deliver me.
Like so many who
have broken their chains,
I want to feel the
pulse in my veins.
The pound
in my heart.
The pressing
of my skin.
The strain
on my art.

Deliver me.
I promise to be me
this time.
I will let them see
the truth that
comes only from deliverance
from passing ways. Wave
me down. Let me stay.

Deliver me.

Dewless Days

My mornings are
surrounded by
chatter.
Footsteps.
Light knocks.
Then heavier.
Mask-wearing,
covered faces with noses poking out.
Protruding.
Cover them,
I say. I am tired.
I now point instead
to my own covered nose.

Copy me.
Enforcer.
Facilitator.
Educator.
Babysitter.
Counselor.
I am all of it.

My mornings are
surrounded by
distant yelps and
laughter. Echoing
through the hallways.
Quiet knocks.
Heavier now. Let me in.
Their eyes
filled with wonder. Anxiety.
I help to ease with
good mornings
and *welcomes*.

My mornings are
surrounded by
quiet moments.
Empty spaces.
Drawn-on whiteboards.
Dry erasers.
I rewrite the dates in large letters.
One more day. The heaviness
of feet dragging on the floor.
Pounding on the door. Let me in.
Shuffling of backpacks.
Smiles behind masks. Tired eyes.
Uncertainty.
They stay three feet apart. But
line up next to one another.

My mornings are
filled with what is next?
Living in the moment,
figuring it out as it comes.
Giving in.
Settling.
Letting go of control.
Taking back when it is time.

My mornings are
filled with duties. Check
emails. Reply back.
Organize. Input
graded work. Grade more.
Create lessons. Check them.
Align.
Reflect.
Repeat.

My mornings are
filled with gratitude
for another day to
try something new. Even
if it is small. To see.
To never feel too comfortable.
To always be me.

My mornings are filled.

Crawl Space

If my heart
could run away from all the hurt.
Skip away
from disappointment's lurk.
Step out of closed doors
to find another open.

If my heart
could be swollen.
Protected from the bumps,
bruises, and scars.
Healed from all the parts,
burned by the tar.

If my heart
could travel to safe keepings.
Keep away
from the hate and beatings.
Angry people
look at you and want to
destroy your heart.

They don't understand the
love I am capable of imparting.
They'd rather see my heart burn
in the fire like all the rest who
rose up and tried to
test life with a smile.

Lost their eyes and
no more trials left. The judge
has made their regrets and
now the heart sits jailed
in a prison box,
no longer beating
or beating too slow to know.

Should I
dismiss my heart forever?
Never give it another shot.
Never try to work through
the place I was caught.

Can't give up
on my heart so easily.
It has places to go and
wonders to see. It still has
work to do.

Set the heart free.

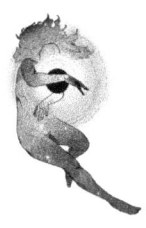

DEAR SPACE TRAVELER,

How far do we journey to wean ourselves off dependency and come into our own unique selves?

The space you've traveled to in this collection is a reflection of many souls. The infinite, existing in and outside of these pages, timeless and immeasurable. From this point on, we are everything and nothing. My most humble discovery, I know nothing, but I can always learn more of it. **Nothingness is the complete breakdown of our existence**. To recognize we exist in the fabrics of the universe as an integral yet microscopic piece, is all too familiar.

Space traveler, you've come this far. Will you settle here or keep exploring?

I am grateful for your bravery, for your choice to be a part of detriment and excitement. All of the loss and gain, hopes and nightmares. You've made it, and I pray you continue on your own inescapable light journey. Remember healing is lifelong — choose it every day.

May God bless you and guide you in your self-discovery.

Signing off,
Wynter L. Eddins

Final Chapter:
SINGULARITY

Acts of Gratitude

Act 1:

Grateful for
"the good."
Grateful for
"the bad."
Grateful for
everything I've had.
Having
is living, not
always giving.
Spending
the moments.

Act 2:

In pain.
In pleasure. To
repeat is insane. I
keep repeating the
same thing.
I keep
seeing.
I keep
looking.
And doing.
Feeling
comfortable.
Feeling
uncomfortable.

Act 3:

Find
growth there.
Find
space there.
Flourish.
Nurture.
Speak to her.
She
is listening.
She
is sitting there,
glistening. To
see her is to
care. To show her
no more despair.
Speak joy unto her.
Shout her pain.
See her.
Call her name.

Infinite Love

To the past.
To the pain.
To the everlasting
feeling of change.

Sweeping over me,
calmly, roughly
changing
the way I am.

I am not
the same person.
I am better
than the old me.

She was
misguided.
She followed
worn out roads.
She was
slighted in her thoughts.
Dampened
and weak. She forgot
who she was.

God's love.

Gave her
a second chance
to step
into her own path.
She chooses to
laugh in hard times.
She pushes
on the grind.
She gives
more these days,
not letting
noise dictate her heart.

She has found
her infinite start.

Illuminate

Shine on.
Color outside the lines.
Step
out of the box.
Now is the time.

Shine on.
Like a new day.
Wipe away the tears.
Let them
fade away.

Shine on.
A radiant light
touches
everything.
Even at night.

Shine on.
Uncover
your heart.
Let it bleed.
Let it be art.

Shine on.
Keep close
to your dreams.
Press on.
Let them be seen.

Shine on.

Warmest Star

Locking
you in again,
I can feel you
in the deepest ocean.

Swim.

Find comfort there.
The darkest parts
are where I shine.
You will find
buried treasures
that tell stories of
when I told mine.

Adventures. Bottled
up inside. Told you to
search for when I was alive
and you found
the message. You read it
out loud. It was destined.
I felt endowed
to my Purpose.

If my pursuit
was not for you,
I would have to try again.
The love I feel is new,
a refreshing
drink of water.
A splash
on my face.
The dirt
washed away.

Saving grace.

Sail on.

Morning Wealth

Break of dawn, get up.
Time to wake up.
Stretch those
sleepy arms to the sky.

Look up and thank God
you are alive. Feet, feel
the coldness of the ground.

Just look around
to hear the hearts of many
stirring around. Ready to
start their day. Sleep-filled
eyes will disappear.

Time to
get on the move.
Blessed to wake up
and groove. Shout for grace
and thankfulness, too.

Glory of life is,
we aren't through.
There is work to do,
seeds to grow. Don't
waste time cursing truths.

Hearts are needed
in our community light.
So, thank God
we made it through the night.
Keep going,
heal the soul.
Never let go of
a beautiful vision. It just takes time
and laser-focused precision.

Press on.
Don't count the losses
and wins. The heart will
flutter, drop, and then begin again.

Embrace the struggle,
the disheartening times.
Pray for others.
It means growth is in line.

Everything you do
causes the world to
shine.

Peace to Will

Armor up
today. Put on
the defense.
It is time to fight
again.

The battle
for peace
is coming for you.
Let down
your shield
to uncover
your truth.

Defend it.
It is time
to fight again.
The battle
for peace
is on the line.

Will you
show up or give up
now? This is the time
to step up. It's
time again
to show up.

Peace
follows
war.

Every heart
must be
restored.

Let us
fight
again.

Peace will always win.

Barrier Matter

Given we are standing here
together, let's connect.
Figure out the reasons
where we may
disconnect. Find some
solutions
to our own tired neglect.

Like a played-out tune,
a washed-up shore,
a tired story
no one wants to hear anymore.
A drawn out speech
misses the floor.

Restructure
the current ideas now.
Don't repeat a story
that tells us how.

How to
navigate our Black bodies.
How to
interact with somebody who
does not look like us.

An insane philosophy to
claim me,
claim my ancestry, say
I must be chained to it.
I must point the blame,
hold anger in my heart.

That is the part
I cannot accept.
Handouts
are what I reject.

To think I am less than
deepens the nonsense well.
Oh well, here we are,
standing next to one another.
Our different skin colors
are all they see. But if
I look into your eyes, there's
a reflection of me.

Infinite Connection

When you pray for me,
please do so in good faith.
Pray for those
who cannot pray for their start.
The beauty of prayer
is it starts in our hearts.

A kindling,
ready to set ablaze.
Pray for those
who wish for better days.
Keep them close to the lips,
heavy on the tongue.

Choose the words gladly.
Don't worry about being
wrong or right. Pray for those
who don't have light. Whose
hearts are too heavy
to dare speak hope.

Let them hear their dreams.
Pray for bountiful means.
God provides in due time.
Keep the promise.
It is mine and yours.
We share together,
joined hands are better.

So when you pray for me,
let it be in truth.
The most beautiful
part of this world
is our youth.

Steer North

I want to ride!
Deep down inside,
I feel alive.
Call upon my soul.
Just let them know
it's a driver's show.

I want to ride!
Front seat this time.
God put me there.
I want to shine!
For my people.
I want to grind.

I want to ride!
Don't divide us.
I have two skins.
I have one Black,
and underneath,
is a white sheath.

I want to ride!
With you alongside.
Together, too.
Let's not divide
by our colors' hue.

I want to ride!
Together on the same horse.
Steering for common cause.
Love is our common call.
Let's fight and give our all.

Galactic Moves

Only way is
forward.
Only way is
through.
This is
nothing new.

Backward
is not an option.
No one can opt in
better than you.
To stand
and get through.

You can.

Only way is
to demand better.
Never give in.
Begin. Start.
Give all your heart.

Have a voice.
Use it.
Don't
abuse it.

Be true to you.

Discover
something new.
Inside, it calls.
Answer it.

Love
never
stalls.

Wild. Honey. Nectar.

Sweeter than blooms
on a freshly picked tree.
More delicious
than the taste of harmony.
Running
through the valley.
Swimming
through the sea.
Climbing
to the mountaintop.
Finding God
by the tree.

Wild. Honey. Nectar.

Flowing
so easily.
Ready
for everyone.
Ready
for you
and me.

Cosmic Forces

I see you
peeking through. Looking
for answers
to not approach.
To stand
on the sidelines. Waiting
for some to see.

I can see you.

Step out of the shadows.
Show your face
for who you really are.
Why care about what they think?

They don't see you
like I do.
They will
walk all over you
if you let them.

Don't.

Show up this time.
Look them in the eyes.
Stop repeating the signs.
Break them.

Hazards.

Take more risk
this time or
else, stay there.
Stuck and lonely,
forever repeating.
Never-ending cycle
of pity and doubt.

No more.
It's time to shout
and let your
voice be heard.
Are you scared of
what they might think?
Kinky hair,
long legs, and a wink.

Use it all.

God-given talents
never fall.
They rise and
build empires. You are
Sire, you are Queen.
You are everything
if you remember.

The love you receive is an ember.
It burns and grows
more brightly in the night.

Feel how you are
burning inside.
Let the fire grow and
begin to warm the ground.
No more looking around,
wondering why.
You know the reason.
Now, you must try.
Now, you must deliver.

Since you can
see what is in store.
You must give it your all.
You must give life more.

Start Energy

I can't go back to the old me.
Shame on you for thinking I would.
Shame on you for thinking I could.

I could not take one step back —
that is way too much.
Jesus Christ saved me.
How could I go back to the old me?

The one who felt shame and unworthiness.
Insecure, I will no longer feel fear,
for Jesus has placed His love in my heart.
I cannot go back to the place where I started.
For it is a new beginning I have embarked on.
This journey is so beautiful.

Why would I go back to the dark?
Why would I travel back to the pain?
Why would I replay this thing that's insane?

I could not even dare myself to think of this,
of putting myself back on the shelf.
I have dusted myself, I have finally won.
My only truth is that I've begun,
so don't even try to drag me back.

Because

I can't go back to the old me.
Shame on you for thinking I would.
Shame on you for thinking I could.

I will not go back.
My place is right here,
building the kingdom.
Stacking to the sky,
I no longer get so high
that I can't even think for myself.
See, they want to numb you,
want you to feel like you
could never be someone else.

They don't want you to claim your power.
Look yourself in the eye —
know that you are worthy and it's okay to cry.
It's okay to fall.

We keep moving,
we keep grooving,
and seeing something bigger.

The heavens are open.
We are closer than we know.
We don't have to give in
because we already got the glow.

God gave us love,
gave us all we need.
We don't have to think about the bounty.
It's already reaped.

Perceive something greater,
We are generational curse-breakers.
Human beings place limits,
but we cannot limit our beings,
for God is inside of you and me.

My heart will continue to rise.
I will continue to touch skies.
Matter of fact, I'm out of this Earth,
beyond in the space,
no longer trying to chase
or race or judge myself
or compare.

No more, no more.

I'm not staying on the floor.
I'm not crying and dying.
I am no longer lying to who I am.
I look myself in the mirror
and tell myself I will win.

I can't go back to the old me.
Shame on you for thinking I would.
Shame on you for thinking I could.

Spacelift

Heavy eyes
pressing down.
Don't close them now.
They're still
calling your name.
Asking you to show up.

Feet feel like
weights tied.
Shackling through this
day to day.
When will I
break away?
From the grind,
the constant time.
Counting minutes
down.

Heads glued to
cellular devices.
No one looks around,
no one looks at you.

They look on through.
Like a ghost,
they can't see me.
I hope they believe me
when I say this is it.
This is the time
where I step away
from this shit.

Wipe the caked
grease from my brow.

Give the finger,
then perform a bow.
Gracefully skip away
from the mess.
Work for pennies
and expect to call it progress.

I learned to
create my own way.
Expect nothing
from no one,
but invest anyway.

Be the change
I want to see.
Live the way
I want to be.
Be better than
I was yesterday.
See my future
and never stray.
Heavy eyes
calling my name.

Time to rest now
on my own spaceplane.

Keep soaring.

Universal Blessings

God's love
is an abundance.
It falls fresh upon
hearts each day.
We can't give in.
We can't stay in the dark.
With God's love,
there is a luminous spark.
Ready to set fire,
the trail ablaze.
The beauty of God's love
is endless days.

Filled up to fulfill the
heart's wildest dreams.
Break through knowing
we are protected.
Embark on the journey
knowing it's reflected.
Keep God close
everywhere we go.
An abundance of love,
a never-ending flow.
Prayer is like having
an open conversation.
God's love connects
and awakens the nations.

Macrocosmic Might

Standing up
when you feel like falling,

that is power.

Speaking up
when you feel like being silent,

that is power.

Showing up
when you feel like disappearing,

that is power.

Pushing on
when you feel like giving in,

that is power.

Holding on
when you feel like letting go,

that is power.

Being strong
when every part of you feels broken,

that is power.

Getting along,
when you feel like telling everyone to "f off,"

that is power.

Paying bills
when you can barely make ends meet,

that is power.

Choosing responsibility
over negativity,

that is power.

Climbing up the mountain
when you feel like sliding down the hill,

that is power.

Swimming
when you feel like sinking,

that is power.

Sacrifice
over gratification,

that is power.

Creating a plan
when you feel like winging it,

that is power.

Having a vision
over daydreaming,

that is power.

Relaxing and resting
when you feel like you have no time,

that is power.

Silence,
sitting still,
listening,

that is power.

Holding space
for others,

that is power.

Challenging
your own beliefs,

that is power.

Being willing
to hear opposing ideas,

that is power.

Never giving in
when you feel like giving up,

that is power.

Being here,
being present,
being real.

That is power,
and you can
access it
now.

Celestial Rebirth

A new birth
from a new day.
Dawn has risen
and called out.

A new name
formed from a renewed lane.
Carved and paved
out under bushes.

A new time,
a fresh mind to sprout.
Ideas blossoming from
a courageous soul.

A new way to deliver,
an alternate way to go.
Break out of the cage
and do not wither.

A new heart,
improved start to show Her
the way, the truth, and the light.
A new path to follow,
let it burn so very bright.

Earth Bounty

Take it all back now.

Each and every piece.
Take it all back now.
The dust under your feet.
Take the broom and sweep.

Take it all back now.

Every pebble,
every rock. Everything
that told you to stop.
Take it all back now.

Return to your power.
Return the hourglass
filled up.
Overfilled with
self-love.

Take it all back now.

The negativity.
Trying to be.
The wanting to be.
The needing to see.

Take it all back now.

The conformity.
The "I am not good enough."
The "unless there's a filter,
I am not pretty enough."

Take it all back now.

The justifications,
the settling,
the losing of self.

Take it all back now.

Demand it all
be refunded fully.
Interest given for
what you did truly.

Take it all back now.

The doubt,
the looking down,
the pity. The shame.
The emptiness.
The lasting pain.

Take it all back now.

Return it with love.
Love is your true calling.
An exchange from above.
Live in your truth
and everything else.

Take
it all
back
now.

Land Sleep

Resting
to build.
Resting
to shield.
Resting
to give more to the world.
Resting
for reflection.
Resting
for collection.

Thoughts
need rest.
Visions
need rest.
Service
needs rest.
Hearts
need rest.
Souls
need rest.
Minds
need rest.

Resting
for energy.
Resting
for synergy.
Resting
to understand.
Resting
to create more plans.

Rest without guilt.

First Steps

No matter
the distance,
the height
and resistance.
You can make it.

No matter
the battle,
the tearing down,
the shackles
broken,
still there holding.
You can make it.

No matter
the uphill.
The constant drill
of work, work, work.
The constant bills that
hurt, hurt, hurt.
You can make it.

No matter
the doubts.
The questioning.
The painful shouts.
The looking down.
The pouts.
You can make it.

No matter
the glory.
The one-time victory.
The untold history.
You can make it.

No matter
the shame.
The buried down pain.
The pieces still remain.
You can make it.

No matter
the teasing.
The looking down.
The aiming to please.
You can make it.

No matter
the cuts,
so deep
in the skin.
The pain doesn't end.
You can make it.

You
can
make it.

But first:

You
must
break it.

Baby steps.

Rocketry

Morning stars
are lighting the sky.
Twinkling
still, even in the light.
I make a wish at sunrise.
Step out
on the horizon to peer.
I know that my time
is near.

Whispering of the wind
is closer.
My heart knows, too.
It's bolder.
Today, she wants to
take a risk.
Like a light, she
scares away
the emptiness.
She lights a path
into the deep.

Light Protector

She picked up this time
and spoke clearly. Remember
when you could hardly hear her?
She would lower her voice in
exchange for fear.
Made it sound lighter,
childlike,
like she couldn't present
her true nature that night.

Robbed.
Stolen.
Taken.

She is still shaken
from that fight.
But she picked up,
despite the constant callings
of her own demons. She sent them
straight to voicemail. She sent them
straight to hell.
She refused to answer them,
but when you called,
she decided she was ready to begin.

She picked up and let you in.
You took her hand so carefully.
She is crying inside still.
She can't believe this is real.
The goodness,
the feeling of happiness
is difficult to accept,
yet you remind her
she does not need to regret.

She can live on.
She can still
sing her songs,
and you will listen.
She needed someone
to hear her screams,
her dreams,
and her nightmares.
To hold her.
To love her.

She did not know it was you,
so she did everything to
destroy the truth.
She walked out.
She stepped away.
She turned a blind eye,
and hoped you would stay.
You did.
Like a fool, she thought.

How could you love someone
who has been caught in the darkness
and drowned in the marshes?
Who danced with a monster?
Yet you still see her
as your dream.

She could not believe you,
but when you called that night,
she knew it was true.
She picked up,
despite her feeling self-hate.

She woke up,
and now you have
changed her ways.

She is better,
and now there are
better days.

Shooting Star

Wishes are finding their way
into my heart again.
Hoping and dancing
and painting the town as they spin.

Wishes are singing their way
into my heart again.
Melodies so sweet,
they awaken my skin.

Wishes are kissing and sipping
on my heart again.
Cups overflowing,
their bellies are filling in.

Wishes keep coming and tumbling
into my heart again.
Jumping and jacking and
speed-driving for the win.

Wishes aren't stopping
but sprinting into my heart again.
Dashing and mashing
and cartoon-splashing in.

I open my heart and say
"Wishes,
let's begin!"

Sword Fight

Take up the sword today.
Pick it up and
look away.
The lies will burn.
The hearts will yearn.

Believe them. Truth
is in her eyes.
Shadows cover banks.
If she sinks,
she dies.

The only way to save her
is to let her save herself.
Let her struggle.
Let her call for help
if she needs it.

The safety vest
tied around her waist
is choking out her breasts.
The air released barely left.
Who did this?

Did she ask to be saved?
Did she wave her hands?
Recognize her bravery.

Slavery, they say.
Her ancestors, they say.
A cycle of poverty, they say.
Must chain her back into it.
To help her succeed
is to push her through it.

She cannot do it.
She cannot do it.
She cannot do it.

On her own.

But she already has.
She already
cut right through
the safety nets you placed.

Traps.
Pits.
Tar.

Shifts.

She already
saw right through it.
Looked into their eyes
and already knew it.
Took up the sword,
sliced away
their protective fluid.
More like a rejection
of compliance
to attempt to
rid a Black woman's silence.

She no longer
plays their games.
Instead, she remembers
her new name.

Her fight is her own.

A community regrown.

Inner Compass

Guide me, oh Lord,
I trust in you
to strengthen my heart
in all that I do.

Call me, oh Lord,
to my purpose and path.
Lead me there,
so I do not stray, alas.

Seek me, oh Lord,
for you are in my heart.
I want you to stay there.
Promise not to part.

Forgive me, oh Lord,
for I have fallen short
time and again.
A failed report
I send.

Embrace me, oh Lord,
Your light is the way.
I surrender to you.
Each and every day.

Screen Glory

God is putting
new glass in the window of my soul.
I see now
I must let go
of any feeling that
won't serve His will.
He looks at us all
and then we sit still.

Watch Him
in awesome glory.
God unified us
under the same story.
No matter
the color of our skin.
We are a people
united within.

Our hearts are woven
in a quilted sheet.
Colorful patterns
make for you and me.
The fabric is
a part of a delicate make.
So rare to find,
so hard to break.
Windows painted,
beautiful stains pressed in.

God is putting
new glass in my broken soul.
Now I am repaired
and I must let go
of any part of my heart
that dismisses another.

I am in this world
to love like my mother.
To give unto others
and protect the youth.
Look at their faces —
they look up to you and me.

God is putting
new windows in our soul

Now, together,
united we must go.

Super Martians

Heroes are
giants in a shell.
Let them rise up,
so they can tell
stories of
hearts that battled hell.

        Heroes are
        giants in a shell.
        Pieces picked up
        by souls that fell.
        Hear the silent screams
        you can yell.

                Heroes are
                giants in a shell.
                Contained by love,
                they can heal.
                Saved a generation
                from shark whales.

                Heroes are giants
                in a shell.

Seismic Shift

Why not start? Today
is your day to
find the way. It is
there for you.

Explore
the world, too. Travel
for miles. Then
smile. Look back
with wonder.
Hold curiosity
and yonder.
Ponder on it.

Dream big
and get anything
you want. Be blunt
and tell them. You are
meant to swim. You may
sink at times.

But that is
temporary.
You will
rise and shine.
You are
glowing now.

Let them
see you grow.
Inside,
your fire is lit. And you
have what they can't get.
Unless you share
everything. Let them
hear you sing.
From the mountaintops,
your voice rings.

You can be
anything.
But first, you must
believe.
There is a ring.
Answer the call.
Life's too
short to stall.

Starburst

Fill up,
you will need it.
The journey is long
and you must fill up.

With vision so strong,
you'll always see it.
Even when they tell you
nothing will come from it.

You will smile,
overfilled with
a vision
from God.

Intergalactic Community

And soon, there will be
a people among you.
there to uphold
and uplift one another.
Suffered so long,
but closed wounds make
for stronger hearts.

The people among you
are no longer there to start
but to finish God's work
and cure
crushed hearts.

Mended,
healed through the process
that creates diamonds.
Pressured under heat,
burned and bruised.
Out from the ashes
comes a people among you,
tightly wrapped and
well-connected.
Resources tapped
to build the vision for the people.

Among you, some have
developed their own provisions.
The youth are innovators
releasing their creations.
Curiosity that builds dreams,
a carnival of nations.
Ideas so colorful
everyone wants to enjoy the ride.

Cotton candy lands of
beautified regions on demand.

A people among you,
united through struggle.
Ready to let go of
anger and resentment.
Ready to build lives
that reflect their inner sentiment.

Their hearts are polished
sequoia wood, too large.
Growing to touch the skies
and beyond. Ready to explore
new galaxies,
focused on shifting and giving.

Soon, the people
among you will rise.
Clouds will no longer rain
acid on their lives.
Give to them what they
have given to this land.

Enrich the soil
they have put much work in.
Yield the crops,
produce new technologies.
Invest in NFTs,
cryptocurrencies,

And soon, there will be
a people among you.

Radiated Pressure

The only way to go is up.

Look at the top.
Will it ever be enough?
Will we set ourselves free?
Or be locked in
a cage of dependency?

Speak kindly on the way.
Give greatness
to the place you stay.
Hold space for her to find a way.
Forgive her often.
She needs you now.

Give time to her
and show her how.
Protect her needs.
Grow and plow,
plant the seeds.
Ask her questions.
Challenge her intellect.

Never. Neglect. Her.

She is always
searching, looking
for something new.
Tell her to slow down.
Tell her to look around.

The only way to go is up.
Remind her of this.
That she is enough.
The spaces she travels
are certainly tough.

Prepare her.
Keep her close.
Remind her
that love is toast.
Lightly burned
to perfection.
She is the
perfect reflection.

Let her
see herself now.
Let her
grow from the ground.
Let her
bloom fully.
Let her
live truly.

The only way to go is up.

Lethargy

Stillness is like
feeling a needle
for the first time.
Like seeing the blood
for the first time.
Like giving in
for the first time.

Stillness is like
the opposite of numbness,
a sensation to feel one's whole body
in place.
To feel your feet.
To feel the defeat,
and let it wash over you.

Like a cleansing rain,
let it pour down,
no matter the pain,
no matter what comes next.

Standing still is like
being on top of a hill and not wanting to jump
for the first time.
Wanting to see
for the first time.
Wanting to be
for the first time.

Letting oneself be free
for the first time.
Not giving in this time.
Not repeating
the same things.
Stillness is like
letting regrets find their rightful place.
It's like feeling it.

Have you ever wanted to feel? All of it,
no matter the subjectiveness,
no matter what is next,
you embrace it.
Hold it tightly,
you can taste it
and hear it.

As clear as train tracks traveling on the click-clacks,
running into paradise.
I hope I see you on that car ride this time,
sitting still.

I hope we can
look each other in the eyes and still feel connected.

Wouldn't that be the best destination?
If we were to travel
in stillness and still arrive where we planned to be?

I will meet you there,
in our destiny.
But first, we must buckle up and enjoy the ride.
Look out the window,
see the sights
and just be still,
just be real,
just accept the feelings.

No more numbness to the pain.
Let it wash over you like the coldest rain,
wash away any shame.

I pray this for you.
I pray that you feel and know your name.

Stillness.

Roomy

Am I more
than I was yesterday?
Did I find another way
or tap at the same corners?
Was I stuck in place?

Am I better
than I was yesterday?
Did I stop to listen?
Did I choose to look down?
Am I giving it all I got?

Do I come out
swinging?
Am I calculated?
Am I messy
with my purpose?
Do I have a vision?

Am I more peaceful
than I was last night?
Did I pray for this?
Did I make way for this?
Lord, am I
moving along okay?

Can you put a name to this?
Am I still the same?
Am I moving
in that direction?
Is this the way?

I want to be
better than I was.

I want to
climb further.
I want to
break barriers.
I want to be
more than I am.

I know that I can.
Through prayer
and practice.

Action
is my name.

Believe

Claim it.

Put your name on it.
Full title it.
Own it.
Stand tall on it.
Be free with it.
Mark an X with it.

Claim it.

Treasure it.
Dig deep for it.
Jump with joy for it.
Clap your hands for it.
Uplift it. Keep it. Forever.
Speak on it.

Claim it.

Be real with it.
Tell the truth to it.
Embrace it.
Celebrate it.
Give more to it.

Claim it.

Be kind to it.
Have high hopes for it.
Love on it.
Remember it.
Empower it.

Claim it.

Want and need it.
Make more of it.
Focus on it.
Drive it.
Full force.
Wake it.

Claim it.

Rest on it.
Open your heart for it.
Promise it.

Claim it.
Claim it.
Claim it.

You

Are

It.

Cosmic Resistance

Two feet planted
loosely in the sand.
Ready to move
and grind into.

Shifting through a new
and better land.
Blood and sweat
mixed in a hue.
Heart gives
then stops then gives more again.

Legs like stilts
tightly in place.
Hurt lingering
inside my Black skin.
Shaking it feels
like fresh mace.
Stinging, burning,
crawling from all sin.

Step close,
look them in the face.
Elements pushing,
screaming again.
Push back, fight,
and find another way.

Healing is the resistance.

North Star

She traveled far
Went off path and was lost
No north star
The price paid really cost

Her feet stuck
Dark marshes drawing her in
Life was muck
How could she ever begin again?

She stood alone
Tears stained under her eyes
Her strength gone
She wept, how many tries?

Kept falling on her knees
God help me
She pleaded to the trees
Peace I see

Silence came over her heart
Stillness, calm
A whisper pierced like a gentle dart
Carry on

She stepped over broken branches
Followed light
Her path back was like avalanches
So tough, a blight

Down the mountain she walked steadily
Legs aching
A familiar sight so close and readily
Painstaking

Now the air was fresh and new
She breathed in
This was her life to pursue
Time to begin

ABOUT THE AUTHOR

Wynter Eddins is a published author from the San Fernando Valley in Los Angeles County. Eddins' poetry showcases the hidden struggles of Black women and women of color, emphasizing the importance of cultivating safe spaces and multicultural communities. Her works encompass historical issues facing women, including domestic violence, child sexual assault, and harassment, and displays resilience in overcoming traumatic situations.

Eddins holds a masters of Science in Education from Mount Saint Mary's University, Los Angeles. Her love of educating youth inspired her to start a nonprofit organization — Simply Youth Institute — that teaches students from underserved communities about financial responsibility and healthy relationships. Through workshops and connections to careers and mentors, young women are able to increase their confidence and build generational wealth.

All of her talents and love for art, including acting and spoken word, are tools toward creating healthier communities where young people and women of color feel empowered to share their voices. Her vision is for everyone to achieve financial stability and live in a state of peace.

Stay connected with Wynter:
    Email: wynterleddins@gmail.com
    Instagram: WynterLauren